Racism

Aladdin Books Ltd 2007

Designed and produced by
Aladdin Books Ltd
2/3 Fitzroy Mews
London W1T 6DF

First published in 2007
by Franklin Watts
338 Euston Road
London NW1 3BH

Franklin Watts Australia
Level 17/207 Kent Street
Sydney NSW 2000

Franklin Watts is a division of Hachette Children's Books.

ISBN 978 0 7496 7495 3

A catalogue record for
this book is available
from the British Library.

Illustrator: Christopher O'Neill

The author, Jen Green, has written extensively for young people
on social issues and other topics.

Dewey Classification:
305.8

Printed in China

Racism

Jen Green

Aladdin / Watts

London • Sydney

Contents

Introduction

These children are in the same class. They come from
different cultures, but they all get on well together.
But a few people treat those from other cultures badly.
This is racism. The children in this book will share
with you some ideas on how to deal with racism.

Racists miss out on many friendships.

Racism can be really hurtful.

Say "NO!" to racism.

What Is Racism?

Last week the class discussed racism. Marcus said that racism is treating someone unfairly because of his or her culture – this means having a different religion or a different way of doing things. Grace said racism is also picking on someone because he or she comes from a different country or has a different skin colour.

Racism can happen anywhere.

Racism is being mean because a person's skin is a different colour.

If someone is rude about a person's culture, he or she is racist.

▶ Name-calling

There are different ways in which people may be racist. It is racist to call a person a rude name or to bully someone, just because he or she comes from a different culture or a different country.

Why is he always calling me names?

Out of my way you *#?ø-**!

◀ Why Can't I Play?

Racism can be ignoring a person or leaving him or her out of a game, just because of the colour of a person's skin or his or her culture. Racists try to make others feel as if they don't belong.

▶ Judging Others!

Deciding what you think about a person before you get to know him or her properly is called prejudice. Racist people decide not to like someone just because of his or her skin colour, religion or culture, or even because of his or her clothes – without even knowing the person!

Story: Being Prejudiced

1 The class was asked to bring food to share, for a picnic in the park.

2 Kim and Jane thought they knew all about the kind of food that Anu ate.

3 In fact, Anu brought pizza. Next time, she brought curry - they all loved it!

Kim and Jane were unfair to Anu.

Kim and Jane were prejudiced. They had fixed ideas about Anu, because of her culture. Racist people are prejudiced. They choose to dislike someone who is different, without getting to know him or her. Kim and Jane felt they were better than Anu because her culture was different from theirs. This is racist. All cultures are equally special.

▶ It's Not Funny

Some racists make fun of the way other people talk, and then say they are just teasing. But it's not teasing if someone ends up feeling hurt or left out. Racism is not funny.

He speaks in a funny voice.

Why can't he talk like us?

Come on, all black people are good at running.

◀ Fixed Ideas

It is racist to have fixed ideas about people who come from the same culture, even if those ideas seem good. Each person is different. Everybody deserves to be treated as if he or she is special.

▶ It's Hurtful

When you get upset, you may use hurtful words rather than telling the person why you are angry with them. Name-calling is unfair. It hurts people and it doesn't solve anything. It's much better to tell the person what they have done to make you angry.

What do you know about racism, Jon?

"I'm Jewish. Last year there was a gang of bullies at school. One day they cornered me and asked me for money. When I said no, they started saying all Jews were mean. A teacher heard and put a stop to it. The bullies were prejudiced about Jewish people and had fixed ideas about me, without even knowing me."

The History Of Racism

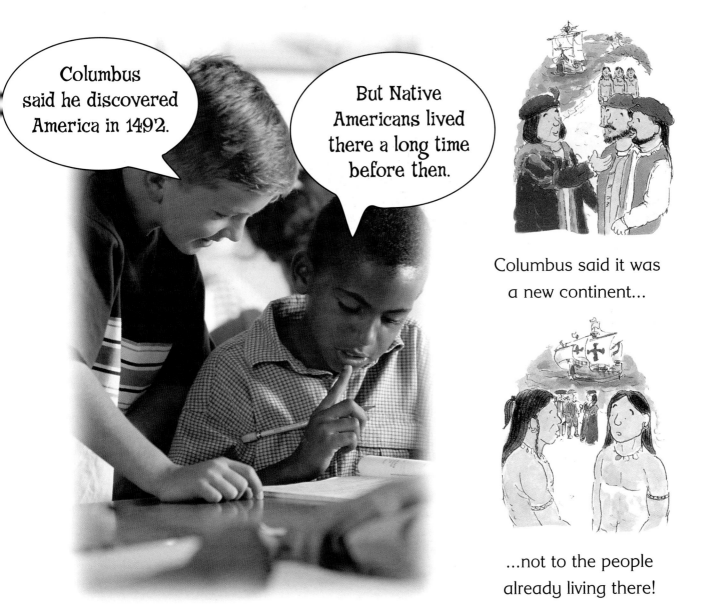

Columbus said he discovered America in 1492.

But Native Americans lived there a long time before then.

Columbus said it was a new continent...

...not to the people already living there!

Paul and Ade are reading a history book. The history of racism goes back a long way. For instance, hundreds of years ago, Europeans travelled to lands where people already lived. They claimed the lands as their own and were unfair to the people who lived there. Racism has affected many people in many different countries.

The History Of Racism

▶ Good Times

Sam's grandparents were born in Germany. But when they were young, they had to leave because a very racist group, called the Nazis, began to attack Jews. Six million Jews were killed by the Nazis, just because they were Jewish. Sam is very proud to be Jewish.

◀ Native Peoples

Nascha is Navajo, one of the first peoples of North America. Around 150 years ago, European settlers in America forced the Navajo off their land and treated them very badly. Nascha enjoys living in modern America but she is also very proud of her Navajo culture. Her name means "owl".

▶ Two Cultures

Jay's grandparents came from Delhi, in India, but he was born in Britain. Indian culture existed for thousands of years, long before British people went there. They treated Indians as if British culture was better than Indian culture. But Jay is proud of both his Indian and British cultures.

Is Ade an African name?

"Yes, it is. It is a Nigerian word meaning "royal". One day, I'd like to visit Jamaica where my parents first lived. My great-great-grandparents were born in Africa. Europeans took them across the sea to Jamaica and made them work there as slaves. But all over the world, people from different cultures won the fight to end slavery."

Racism Today

Katie and Jamila are looking at a globe. Jamila is showing Katie how she travelled from her country, Sudan, to Britain. Jamila is a refugee. Refugees are people who are forced to leave their countries because of war or disaster. Many wars are caused by racists stirring up hatred between people.

We can't stay here, it's not safe.

Why did your parents leave your country?

Because of a war caused by racists.

Story: Repeating Remarks

1 Mike's big sister, Jane, did not like the Indian family across the road.

2 Jane was prejudiced about Indian people. She complained about them to Mike.

3 Later Mike repeated Jane's racist remarks to Ranjit. Ranjit was upset.

Why did Mike hurt Ranjit?

Mike repeated what Jane had said, without thinking. If he had thought about it, he would not have said unfair things. For Ranjit and the Indian family opposite, home is here. They have every right to be here. Racist ideas are learnt from others. If friends or members of your family are racist, try to think for yourself. Tell them what you think.

▲ Green Or Yellow?

Racism divides people into groups based on culture or skin colour. Dividing people in this way is as silly as saying you can only play with others wearing the same colour shirt as you. But we all belong to one race – the HUMAN RACE!

◀ Racism Is Always Wrong

Anyone can be racist, whatever his or her skin colour, religion or culture. Sometimes people blame those from other cultures for problems in the world. This is unfair and not true. There is never any excuse for racism.

Katie, have you ever been in a gang?

"I was in Jake's gang. It was great at first but then some people in the gang started being nasty about Jamila and my African friends. I didn't want to be nasty to Jamila, but I was scared to tell Jake he was wrong. In the end, I told Jake what I thought of him. I left his gang. I'm really glad I did, and now Jamila is my good friend."

Racism Today

▶ Unfair Treatment

A person may be stopped from getting a job or a place at school because of his or her skin colour or culture. This is racism. It is against the law, but it can take a long time to change people's ideas.

▲ Gangs

It can be fun to be in a gang. But it is not fun if there are racist bullies in a gang. Racist gangs attack people from different cultures or pick fights with other gangs.

▶ Hope For The Future

Things can change however. In South Africa, white people tried to rule black people using racist laws, under a system called apartheid. This system ended in 1990. Since then, former President Nelson Mandela and other politicians in South Africa have tried to make sure that everybody is treated fairly.

Feelings

Aaron and Phoebe are talking about how it feels when someone is racist. Aaron said when Jake picked on him, he lay awake at night, and had nightmares when he did fall asleep. Phoebe had to leave her country quickly because of the war there, caused by racists. When she first came here she felt lonely and sad.

Racism can make you worry.

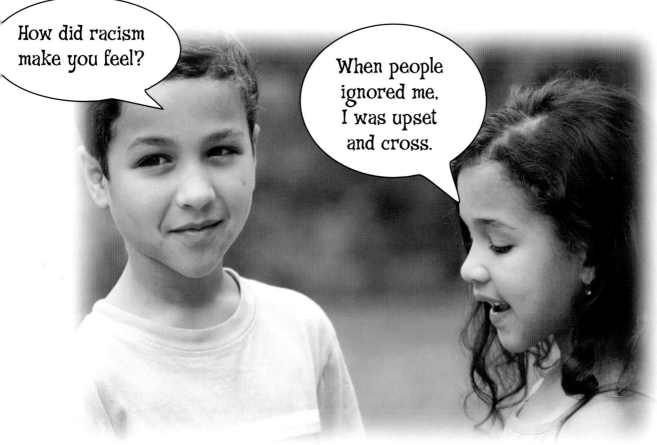

How did racism make you feel?

When people ignored me, I was upset and cross.

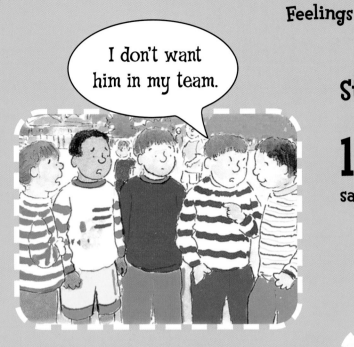

I don't want him in my team.

Story: Speaking Up

1 Paul and Ken were whispering. Tess heard them say racist things about Craig.

Paul and Ken were mean to Craig today.

2 Later Tess told her mum what had happened at school. Tess was upset.

I was scared he'd pick on me if I said anything.

3 Tess didn't like what Paul had said, but felt too scared to speak up for Craig.

Why did Tess feel unsure?

Tess felt unhappy about the way Ken and Paul had acted, but felt too scared to say anything. It takes courage to speak out about something you feel is wrong. If you notice someone being racist, try not to ignore it. Think how you feel when someone is rude to you and everyone else ignores the situation.

▶ Feeling Low

Racist jokes and comments are very upsetting. They can make you feel miserable and lonely. You might feel sick or find it hard to eat properly. If racism happens at school, it might make you want to stay away from school.

◀ Keep Calm

Racism may make you feel angry. You might want to be racist too, or start a fight. It's OK to feel angry, but fighting back is not the answer. It can get you into trouble and doesn't stop the racism. It is better to tell a grown-up you trust.

▶ It's Not Your Fault

If someone is racist to you, it can make you feel unhappy. It might be hard to concentrate at school. But remember it is not your fault if someone is being racist. There is nothing wrong with you – it's the racist who is wrong.

▶ Big Or Small

Racism can make you feel sad and unsure
of yourself. But try to remember all the
things about yourself that you really like.
Feeling good about yourself will help you
to deal with racist remarks.

◀ Talking It Over

If someone has been racist, it will
help to talk about it to someone
you trust. Keeping your feelings to
yourself won't help. Try talking to
your best friend, your mum, dad,
carer or a teacher.

▶ Feeling At Home

When children arrive in a new
country, everything is very
strange. It can take a while before
they learn the new language.
People in their class may ignore
them. This is unfair and makes
them feel scared or angry – they
haven't done anything wrong. If
there are any new pupils from
other countries in your class, try to
make them feel at home. Perhaps
they would like to be in your team.

Yasmin, how did racism affect you?

"A few girls at school called me names after the terrorist attacks on New York. My mum and dad thought about sending me to a Muslim school but I had lots of friends and didn't want to leave. So they went to see my head teacher with some of the other parents. There was a class discussion and we talked about my religion, Islam. It was good to explain what being a Muslim is really about. I think it helped other pupils to understand."

Stopping Racism

Tony, Gary and Connie are talking about how to deal with racism. Connie says you could try ignoring people who are being racist. They might give up if they don't manage to upset you. Tony says he and Gary stood up to Jake when he was being racist and that worked. But sometimes the best thing to do is to tell a grown-up.

Say "No!" to racism.

Di and her friends keep picking on me.

Story: Hitting Back

1 Meera told her teacher that she was being bullied.

I want to talk to you all in my office.

2 Mrs Bird knew where the gang played. She caught them bullying Meera.

You wouldn't like it if someone bullied you like that.

3 Mrs Bird talked to the gang. They realised that they had been unkind.

Was Meera right to tell?

Yes. Sometimes you will need help to deal with racism. Tell a grown-up you trust. He or she may be able to sort things out, without anyone knowing you have told. If the first person you tell can't help, tell someone else. People who are being racist need to understand that their actions hurt other people. They need to be stopped.

Story: Lee Helps Out

1 Karl was German. Tim and Dave always teased him. This time Lee was there.

Karl's got a silly voice.

Don't be so mean!

2 Lee stood up for Karl. He told Dave and Tim to leave Karl alone.

Why do they do that?

It makes me so cross.

3 Karl was pleased that Lee had stood up for him.

Was Lee right to help Karl?

Yes. If you see someone being racist, try to help. Doing nothing is not the answer – it will look as if you agree with what the racists say. If people think they can get away with being racist, they will carry on. If you are not sure how to deal with the problem on your own, ask a grown-up who will be able to help sort things out.

▶ Racism Is Bad For Everyone!

Racists miss out on lots of fun and friends, just because they decide about people without getting to know them. If you take the trouble, you may find that you have lots in common with someone from a different culture.

◀ Enjoy Life!

Instead of being scared of differences, you can share and enjoy them! Every little effort that you make to stop racism will make a difference.

Connie, what can be done about racism?

"My class discussed racism. Some people were surprised to find out how upsetting it can be. We all agreed not to let racism happen in our class. We said we would try to help if we saw anyone being racist. Now, when a new girl or boy arrives in our class we look after them and make them feel welcome."

Don't Forget...

1

How can you deal with racism, Ade?

"It's not easy, but there are things you can do. Try to keep calm. Think carefully about the situation. Sometimes, it's better to walk away. At other times it's best to tell a grown-up. Sometimes, you might be able to tell the racist to leave you alone. Try practising what you're going to say first."

2

What do you think about racism, Yasmin?

"Racists miss out on lots of friendships, just because of their silly ideas about people. We know it's hard, but try not to let racists make you feel unhappy. Tell your good friends how you feel. Good friends help you feel good."

How does your school deal with racism, Jon?

"Our school is very strict about racism. We all agreed that our school should be a safe place for everyone. We don't allow racism to carry on because it affects everyone, whatever his or her culture. We all have a right to feel happy."

Is it right to tell a grown-up about racism, Katie?

"It's not telling tales to talk to a grown-up about racism. It's often the best thing to do, especially if you feel unsure about dealing with a difficult situation on your own. Tell a teacher, a playground helper, your mum, dad or carer. Racism is wrong. It's important that we all try to stop racism."

Find Out More About Racism

Helpful Addresses and Phone Numbers

Talking about problems can really help. If you can't talk to someone close to you, then try ringing one of these organisations:

Childline
Tel: 0800 1111
A 24-hour free helpline for children. The number won't show up on a telephone bill.

Kidscape
2 Grosvenor Gardens,
London SW1W 0DP
Tel: 020 7730 3300 (Mon-Fri 10am-4pm). A helpline for parents of bullied or bullying children. Send a large SAE for copies of their booklets.

Commission for Racial Equality
201-211 Borough High St
London SE1 1GZ
Tel: 020 7939 0000
A good source of information on racism in Britain.

Kids Helpline, Australia
Tel: 1800 55 1800
A 24-hour free helpline for children. Kids Helpline also offers online counselling either via the web or email at www.kidshelp.com.au.

Racism No Way!
Locked Bag 53
Darlinghurst NSW 2010
A project to help schools tackle racism in Australia.

On the Web

These websites are also helpful. You can get in touch with some of them using email:

www.britkid.org

www.teenissues.co.uk

www.childline.org.uk/racism.asp

www.supportline.org.uk

www.youthinformation.com

www.racismnoway.com.au

www.australiansagainstracism.org

www.sikhkids.com

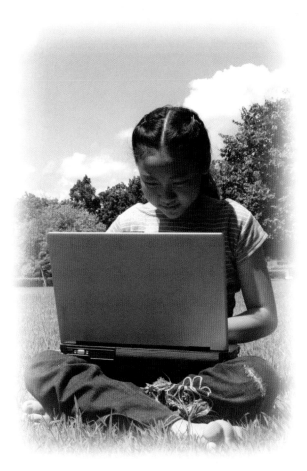

Further Reading

If you want to read more about racism, try:

Talking About: Racism
by Bruce Sanders (Aladdin/Watts)

Choices and Decisions: Dealing with Racism by Pete Sanders and Steve Myers (Aladdin/Watts)

What's That Got to Do With Me?: Racism by Antony Lishak (Franklin Watts)

Everyday Racism
by Annie S. Barnes (Barnes)

What Do We Think About: Racism
by Jen Green (Hodder Wayland)

Get Wise: Racism and Prejudice
by Jane Bingham (Heinemann)

Index

Photocredits

l-left, r-right, b-bottom, t-top, c-centre, m-middle

All photos from istockphoto.com except: Cover tl , 24, 27 — DAJ.

11, 13, 16 — Brand X Pictures. 14 , 17 — Select Pictures/Marc Arundale.

All the photos in this book have been posed by models.